THE NATIONAL PERFORMANCE REVIEW

THE NATIONAL PERFORMANCE REVIEW

HAROLD C. RELYEA, MARCIELE J. CORNEJO RIEMANN
AND HENRY B. HOGUE

Novinka
New York

Senior Editors: Susan Boriotti and Donna Dennis
Coordinating Editor: Tatiana Shohov
Office Manager: Annette Hellinger
Graphics: Wanda Serrano
Editorial Production: Jennifer Vogt, Matthew Kozlowski, Jonathan Rose
and Maya Columbus
Circulation: Ave Maria Gonzalez, Vera Popovic, Luis Aviles, Melissa Diaz,
Vladimir Klestov and Jeannie Pappas
Communications and Acquisitions: Serge P. Shohov
Marketing: Cathy DeGregory

Library of Congress Cataloging-in-Publication Data

Relyea, Harold.
  The National Performance Review / Harold C. Relyea, Marciele J. Cornejo Riemann and Henry B. Hogue.
     p. cm.
     Includes index.
     ISBN: 1-59033-459-0.
     1. National Performance Review (U.S.) 2. Administrative agencies—United States—Cost control. 3. Administrative agencies—United States—Management. 4. Government productivity—United States. I. Cornejo Riemann, Marciele J. II. Hogue, Henry B. III. Title.

JK421 .R4594 2002
352.3'5'0973—dc21

2002033663

Copyright © 2002 by Novinka Books, An Imprint of
         Nova Science Publishers, Inc.
         400 Oser Ave, Suite 1600
         Hauppauge, New York 11788-3619
         Tele. 631-231-7269   Fax 631-231-8175
         e-mail: Novascience@earthlink.net
         Web Site: http://www.novapublishers.com

All rights reserved. No part of this book may be reproduced, stored in a retrieval system or transmitted in any form or by any means: electronic, electrostatic, magnetic, tape, mechanical photocopying, recording or otherwise without permission from the publishers.

The publisher has taken reasonable care in the preparation of this book, but makes no expressed or implied warranty of any kind and assumes no responsibility for any errors or omissions. No liability is assumed for incidental or consequential damages in connection with or arising out of information contained in this book.

This publication is designed to provide accurate and authoritative information with regard to the subject matter covered herein. It is sold with the clear understanding that the publisher is not engaged in rendering legal or any other professional services. If legal or any other expert assistance is required, the services of a competent person should be sought. FROM A DECLARATION OF PARTICIPANTS JOINTLY ADOPTED BY A COMMITTEE OF THE AMERICAN BAR ASSOCIATION AND A COMMITTEE OF PUBLISHERS.

Printed in the United States of America

CONTENTS

Preface		vii
Introduction		ix
Chapter 1	The National Performance Review: Phase I	**1**
	The NPR Report	3
	Implementing the NPR Recommendations	4
Chapter 2	NPR and the 104th Congress: Phase II	**9**
	The First NPR Status Report	10
	The New Republican Congress	13
	NPT Enters Phase II	15
	The Budget Impasse	19
	First-Term NPR	19
Chapter 3	NPT Renewed: Phase III	**21**
	Reinventing the Reinvention Effort	21
	Performance-Based Organizations	26
	The Report Cards and Beyond	29
Chapter 4	Successes, Problems, and Remaining Questions	**33**
	Successes	33
	Problems	38
	Remaining Questions	41
	Closure	45
Index		**47**

PREFACE

Shortly after his inauguration in 1993, President William Clinton announced he was initiating a National Performance Review (NPR) to be conducted over the next six months by a task force headed by Vice President Albert Gore, Jr. In September 1993, this task force delivered a report to the President, offering some 380 major recommendations concerning management reform, reorganization, and government downsizing. Implementation of these recommendations was to be accomplished through presidential directives, congressional action, and individual agency initiatives.

A year later, in September 1994, the NPR issued a status report indicating that 90% of its initial recommendations were being implemented; $46.9 billion of its $108 billion in projected savings had been enacted; an additional $16 billion in savings was pending before Congress; and federal employment had dropped by 71,000 positions. Shortly after the release of this report, the November 1994 congressional elections gave the Republicans majority party control of the House and the Senate for the 104th Congress. Republican leaders had unveiled a *Contract with America* reform plan in late September 1994. Its core principles regarded the federal government as being too big, too expensive, unresponsive to the citizenry, and the perpetrator of burdensome regulations. Consequently, two distinct agendas for reforming and restructuring the federal government were before the 104th Congress. At its conclusion, both the President and Republican congressional leaders could claim some victories in downsizing government. No department was eliminated, however, and only a few small agencies were abolished.

Additional NPR status reports, recommendations, and proposals followed in 1996, 1997, and 1998. Republican congressional majorities continued during the 105th and 106th Congresses. Administration and congressional reinvention and reform efforts resulted in moderate accomplishments during the 105th Congress. Significant exceptions were the overhaul of the structure and operations of the Internal Revenue Service and the consolidation of the foreign policy agencies, both of which were realized as a result of cooperation between the Clinton Administration and Republican congressional leaders. With the convening of the 106th Congress, it appeared that the momentum for pursuing major government reinvention and reform had considerably slowed. The NPR ceased operations with the conclusion of the Clinton Administration on January 19, 2001.

This book reviews the record of the National Performance Review and its 1998 successor, the National partnership for Reinventing Government. It chronicles, as well, related and sometimes competing government reform efforts, and assesses the overall record of the NPR.

INTRODUCTION

During the 20th century, major attempts have been made from time to time to improve the operation of the federal government – largely the program activities of the executive departments and agencies – through management reforms, reorganization, and downsizing.[1] One of the more recent efforts was spearheaded by the Executive Committee of the President's Private Sector Survey on Cost Control of the Federal Government, established by President Ronald Reagan with E.O. 12369 of June 30, 1982. Chaired by industrialist J. Peter Grace, the panel, which became popularly known as the Grace Commission, was composed of 161 corporate executives and was, according to the chartering order, to "advise the President and the Secretary of Commerce, and other Executive agency heads with respect to improving management and reducing costs."[2] Utilizing 36 task forces and the assistance of some 2,000 business executives, managers, experts, and special consultants, the Grace Commission, in January 1984, issued a 467-volume report, with a two-volume summary, which offered 2,478 recommendations.[3] A month later, a General Accounting Office (GAO) and Congressional Budget Office (CBO) joint assessment of a sample of these recommendations resulted in the following GAO conclusions:

---

[1] Generally, see Peri E. Arnold, Making the Managerial Presidency, 2nd edition (Lawrence, KS: University Press of Kansas, 1998); Herbert Emmerich, Federal Organization and Administrative Management (Tuscaloosa, AL: University of Alabama Press, 1971); Paul C. Light, The Tides of Reform (New Haven, CT: Yale University Press, 1997); U.S. Library of Congress, Congressional Research Service, Reorganizing the Executive Branch in the Twentieth Century: Landmark Commissions, by Ronald C. Moe, CRS Report 92-293 GOV (Washington: Mar. 19, 1992).
[2] See 3 C.F.R., 1982 Comp., pp. 190-192.
[3] The Grace Commission's final summary report was commercially published as President's Private Sector Survey on Cost Controls, War on Waste (New York: Macmillan, 1984).

Specifically, of the 396 recommendations assessed, GAO identified 242 as having some merit, 83 as not having merit, and 71 for which GAO had no basis for an opinion. Of the 242 recommendations GAO believed had merit, it had previously made similar or related recommendations in 150 cases. It is important to note, however, that many of the recommendations that do not have merit in GAO's opinion were among those with large savings estimates in the [Grace Commission] reports. It is also important to note that GAO does not agree that all of the proposals for which CBO estimated budgetary savings are feasible or desirable. Conversely, GAO believes that many proposals for which CBO was not able to estimate budgetary savings have merit and deserve further consideration.[4]

While controversy has continued to attend estimates of savings accruing from the implementation of Grace Commission proposals, the Office of Management and Budget (OMB) indicated that 83% of "the unduplicated Grace Commission recommendations have been accepted by the President and reflected in the 1990 or prior budgets."[5]

Among the themes that Arkansas Governor William Clinton brought to the presidency a few years later was the pledge "to radically change the way government operates – to shift from top-down bureaucracy to entrepreneurial government that empowers citizens and communities to change our country from the bottom up."[6] Some of his proposals in this regard,[7] such as

---

[4] U.S. Congressional Budget Office and U.S. General Accounting Office, Analysis of the Grace Commission's Major Proposals for Cost Control (Washington: GPO, 1984), p. 2.

[5] U.S. Office of Management and Budget, Management of the United States Government: Fiscal Year 1990 (Washington: GPO, 1989), p. 5-2.

[6] Bill Clinton and Al Gore, Putting People First: How We Can All Change America (New York: Times Books, 1992), p. 24.

regulating post-employment lobbying activities by senior administration appointees,[8] reducing administrative expenses,[9] eliminating 100,000 federal employee positions,[10] and cutting Executive Office of the President staff by 25%,[11] were partly or fully implemented shortly after his January 1993 inauguration.

---

[7] See ibid., pp. 25-26.
[8] See E.O. 12834, in Federal Register, vol. 58, Jan. 22, 1993, pp. 5911-5916
[9] See E.O. 12837, in ibid, Feb. 12, 1993, pp. 8205-8206.
[10] See E.O. 12839, in ibid, p. 8515.
[11] Ann Devroy, "Clinton Announces Cut in White House Staff," Washington Post, Feb. 10, 1993, pp. A1, A7; Thomas L. Friedman, "Clinton Trimming Lower-Level Aides," New York Times, Feb. 10, 1993, pp. A1, A20. Also see U.S. Library of Congress, Congressional Research Service, President Clinton's Proposed Reduction in White House Staff, by Rogelio Garcia, CRS Report 93-476 GOV (Washington: May 6, 1993).

Chapter 1

THE NATIONAL PERFORMANCE REVIEW: PHASE I

A more ambitious and far-reaching effort at changing government operations was announced by President Clinton on March 3, 1993. He indicated he was initiating a National Performance Review (NPR) to be conducted over the next six months by a task force headed by Vice President Albert Gore, Jr. "Our goal," said the President, "is to make the entire Federal Government both less expensive and more efficient, and to change the culture of our national bureaucracy away from complacency and entitlement toward initiative and empowerment. We intend to redesign, to reinvent, to reinvigorate the entire National Government."[1]

Based upon a similar 1991-1992 assessment in the State of Texas, the NPR was to be assisted by senior department and agency managers, auditors, and front-line workers; OMB management analysts; advice from federal employees, citizens, and private sector leaders; and congressional proposals for eliminating waste in government. The effort was to evaluate the efficiency of every federal program and service; identify specific spending cuts that could be made in federal programs and services not operating effectively and no longer advancing the mission they were intended to serve; recommend ways to streamline the bureaucracy by eliminating unnecessary layers of management and reducing duplication of effort; and find ways to improve services by making better use of new information technology and by making government programs more responsive to the clientele they serve.

---

[1] Weekly Compilation of Presidential Documents, vol. 29, Mar. 8, 1993, p. 350.

In brief, the objective of the NPR was to "reinvent government" – a phrase taken from the popular 1992 book *Reinventing Government*.[2]

By early April, the NPR was organized with 11 "system reinvention" teams and 22 agency-by-agency redesign teams. The former included units on mission-driven, results-oriented budgeting; transforming organizational structures; reinventing personnel management; reengineering through information technology; improving financial management; eliminating internal barriers; improving regulatory systems; empowering state and local governments; rethinking program design; redesigning management systems; and minimizing federal damage to the environment.

Agency-by-agency redesign teams were constituted for each of the 14 Cabinet-level departments and seven specific independent agencies,[3] plus one for all other executive entities. OMB was covered by the budgeting and management systems reinvention teams; the Office of Personnel Management (OPM) was examined by the personnel management reinvention team; and the General Services Administration was scrutinized by the internal barriers reinvention team.

The work of the NPR was formally inaugurated on April 15, 1993, with an assembly that was addressed by Vice President Gore; David Osborne, coauthor of *Reinventing Government*; and Robert Stone, Defense Department deputy assistant secretary for installations and project director for the NPR. As scheduled, NPR personnel, most of whom were agency detailees, gathered information during April and May, and analysis commenced the following month. Recommendations were formulated in July, and drafts of findings and recommendations were circulated to Cabinet members for comment in August.

---

[2] David Osborne and Ted Gaebler, Reinventing Government (Reading, MA: Addison-Wesley, 1992).

[3] These seven agencies were the Environmental Protection Agency, National Aeronautics and Space Administration, National Science Foundation, Nuclear Regulatory Commission, Agency for International Development, Federal Emergency Management Agency, and Small Business Administration.

THE NPR REPORT

The initial NPR report, *From Red Tape to Results: Creating a Government That Works Better & Costs Less*, was delivered to the President on September 7, 1993.[4] Various accompanying supplemental reports on both specific agencies and functional areas of government were subsequently published during 1994. All of these documents and later NPR materials are available through the NPR website, which is now in archival status ([http://govinfo.library.unt.edu/npr/default.html]).

Offering over 380 major recommendations by agency and by affected governmental systems, the initial report also provided a summary of anticipated savings deriving from these recommendations. Unlike several previous presidential study panels on government reform, the NPR did not emphasize executive reorganization in its recommendations, though it did propose that Congress should restore the President's authority to restructure the executive branch through reorganization plans and did suggest over a dozen specific reorganizations.[5] Most of the NPR recommendations sought to streamline government operations, to improve management, and to promote efficiency and economy in administration – all with a view to better service delivery and customer satisfaction. The Grace Commission had some similar recommendations, but made its offerings to combat waste, fraud, and abuse in government.

The mission and initial report of the NPR prompted some critical reaction from the scholarly community concerning the application of some private sector criteria to essentially different public sector enterprises. One public administration scholar objected to the NPR endowing entrepreneurial government with "empowered customers," competition, markets, reduced regulations, charging fees and making money, decentralization, and

---

[4] See Office of the Vice President, From Red Tape to Results: Creating a Government That Works Better & Costs Less. Report of the National performance Review (Washington: Sept. 7, 1993).

[5] The President's authority to prepare reorganization plans and submit them for congressional approval was initially established temporarily in 1939, and was then renewed periodically a dozen times between 1945 and 1984, with slightly varying procedural and plan content conditions. Modification of this authority was made necessary in 1983 when the Supreme Court, in the Chadha case (462 U.S. 919), effectively invalidated continued congressional reliance upon the mechanism of a concurrent resolution to disapprove a proposed reorganization plan. Under the Reorganization Act Amendments of 1984, signed by President Reagan on Nov. 8, 1984, several significant changes were made in the reorganization plan law (5 U.S.C. 901-912 (1988)). These amendments, however, continued the President's reorganization plan authority only to the end of the year, when it automatically expired. President Reagan did not request its reauthorization, nor did President George Bush or President Clinton.

privatization. He cautioned that "promises of better government for less money are simplistic and misleading, regardless of the 'principles' upon which they are based"; "governments are not markets"; "citizens are not customers...they are the owners;" "it is incorrect to assume that either those who work for government or the system of government work are the primary problems"; and "downsizing, rightsizing, cutback management and the other means of reducing the size and costs of government, when combined with deregulation, have significantly diminished the capacities of some units of government to function effectively."[6]

A former Bureau of the Budget specialist in government organization and management observed that contracting government services for private sector performance was not "necessarily cheaper, more efficient and more flexible," and warned:

> Contracting out does not de facto reduce the size of government, promote efficiency, reduce costs or limit the scope of government responsibility. Nor does it eliminate the need for public management; it only changes its character. Because so much of government is contracted out, we urgently need innovation and the development of new approaches to public management. Thus far, we have tended to view the government's role as limited to that of a contract writer and negotiator, auditor and bill payer.[7]

IMPLEMENTING THE NPR RECOMMENDATIONS

To pursue its many recommendations, the NPR proposed the creation of a President's Management Council to "ensure that quality management principles are adopted, processes are reengineered, performance is assessed, and other National Performance Review recommendations are implemented."[8] Subsequently established by a presidential memorandum of October 1, 1993, the council was composed of the chief operating officers of 15 major departments and agencies, representatives of the Administrator of General Services and the director of OPM, and the President's secretary of the Cabinet, with the OMB deputy director for management as the chair.[9]

---

[6] H. George Frederickson, "Painting Bull's-Eyes Around Bullet Holes," Governing, vol. 6, October 1992, p. 13.
[7] Harold Seidman, "Reinventing the Wheel, Not Government," Government Executive, vol. 25, April 1993, p. 32.
[8] Office of the Vice President, From Red Tape to Results: Creating a Government That Works Better & Costs Less, p. 89.
[9] 3 C.F.R. 1993 Comp., pp. 788-791.

Shortly after receiving the initial NPR report, President Clinton began implementing its recommendations. For example, with a memorandum of September 9, 1993, he created the Community Enterprise Board, with the Vice President as chair and 17 other top officials as members, to assist with the implementation of legislation mandating the establishment of empowerment zones, enterprise communities, and rural development investment areas.[10]

NPR recommendations also received attention in the Treasury, Postal Service, and General Government Appropriations Act, 1994, which removed full time employee equivalent floors for some federal agencies funded by the legislation, directed the Internal Revenue Service and U.S. Customs Service to submit plans for restructuring each agency to the Committees on Appropriations, and allowed agencies funded by the legislation to carry over 50% of such unobligated funds for an additional year, with the other half reverting to the Treasury.[11]

The NPR reform effort received added momentum with the October 7, 1993, announcement of the formation of a bipartisan reinventing government study group of House freshmen, cochaired by Representatives Jane Harman (D-CA) and Ken Calvert (R-CA). Calling the NPR report "an important first step in laying out specific proposals for reducing government waste and cutting red tape," organizers of the group called upon the Speaker and other House leaders to schedule votes on NPR proposals during the remaining months of the 103rd Congress.[12] President Clinton provided the opportunity for a major vote in this regard when, on October 26, 1993, he transmitted to Congress a proposal implementing a number of NPR recommendations, including reorganization of the Department of Agriculture and U.S. Army Corps of Engineers, streamlining of the Department of Housing and Urban Development, and termination of the Alaska Power Administration, the Uniformed Services University of the Health Sciences, and various individual programs. On October 28, the measure was introduced as the Government Reform and Savings Act of 1993 (H.R. 3400), and portions were referred to 17 committees for a period ending not later than November 15, 1993. Ten of these panels reported and the other were discharged from further consideration of the bill on November 15. The House Committee on Rules held a November 19 hearing on the bill and reported a modified

---

[10] See Weekly Compilation of Presidential Documents, vol. 29, Sept. 13, 1993, pp. 1716-1718.
[11] See 107 Stat. 1226.
[12] Office of Representative Ken Calvert, "Calvert Calls for Votes This Session on Reinvention Proposals," press release, Oct. 7, 1993; Karen Foerstel, "Frosh Join Call for Vote This Session on Gore Plan," Roll Call, Oct. 7, 1993, pp. 3, 18.

version of it the following day.[13] Floor discussion commenced on November 22, and the House subsequently approved H.R. 3400, as amended, on a 429-1 recorded vote.[14] The bill was referred to the Senate, and the first session of the 103rd Congress concluded on November 26.

With the beginning of the second session of the 103rd Congress in late January 1994, some Senate committees began examining portions of H.R. 3400, but the bill was formally referred only to the Committee on Governmental Affairs. A hearing was held by that committee on February 23 to consider those sections of H.R. 3400 within its jurisdiction. Testimony was received from Comptroller General Charles Bowsher and OMB Deputy Director Alice Rivlin. On March 23, the committee voted to report a new bill (S. 2170) addressing only four of the 17 titles of H.R. 3400. The committee's report accompanying the new bill commented that, "Senate action on the entire H.R. 3400 will most certainly depend on the action taken by other committees with regard to those provisions within their jurisdiction."[15] However, no other Senate committee moved any of the other titles of H.R. 3400 for Senate floor consideration during the second session. The Senate eventually considered and passed S. 2170 in late September and the House gave its approval to the bill in early October, clearing the measure for the President's signature on October 13, the result being a modest implementation of NPR recommendations.[16]

That same day, President Clinton also approved two other bills implementing NPR recommendations. Reform of government procurement arrangements was accomplished with the Federal Acquisition Streamlining Act.[17] Presidential directives facilitating the implementation of the new law were coincidently issued when it was signed.[18] The other approved legislation, originally a federal crop insurance reform bill, had been amended to reorganize the Department of Agriculture.[19]

Several months earlier, on March 30, 1994, President Clinton had signed another measure, the Federal Workforce Restructuring Act, implementing an

---

[13] U.S. Congress, House Committee on Rules, Providing for Consideration of H.R. 3400, 103rd Cong., 1st sess., H.Rept. 103-403 (Washington: GPO, 1993).
[14] See Congressional Record, vol. 139, Nov. 22, 1993, pp. 31990-31991.
[15] U.S. Congress, Senate Committee on Governmental Affairs, Government Management Reform Act of 1994, report to accompany S. 2170, 103rd Cong., 2nd sess., S.Rept. 103-281 (Washington: GPO, 1994), p. 2.
[16] 108 Stat. 3410.
[17] 108 Stat. 3243.
[18] See E.O. 12931 and a related presidential memorandum of Oct. 13, 1994, in 3 C.F.R., 1994 Comp., pp. 925-926, 1040.
[19] 108 Stat. 3178.

NPR recommendation.[20] It authorized the departments and agencies to begin a downsizing of their personnel through early retirement buyouts. Another law, the Government Performance and Results Act, given presidential approval on August 3, 1993, was recommended in the initial NPR report and the legislation had been endorsed by President Clinton when it was introduced in the 103rd Congress.[21] The proposal, however, predated the NPR and had been largely developed by Senator William V. Roth, Jr. (R-DE).

---

[20] 108 Stat. 111.
[21] 107 Stat. 285.

Chapter 2

NPR AND THE 104TH CONGRESS: PHASE II

With the issuance of its first status report and the Republican takeover of the House in the fall of 1994, NPR transitioned into a second phase of goals and activity. This change in goals put the reinventing effort on a parallel track with the reform efforts advocated in the *Contract with America*, which formed the cornerstone of the agenda of the new Republican majority in Congress. Reform advocates in both branches focused on defining the appropriate scope of government functions, rather than *how* government should function, which had been the question undergirding Phase I of the NPR. The NPR claimed that Phase I, in the executive branch, had been very successful, and laid out the agenda for a second phase with new recommendations for saving money, modifying or ending programs, and privatizing some government functions. The House Republican leadership, under Speaker Newt Gingrich, pushed for passage of *Contract* legislation, including bills to reduce the size and scope of government. Although both branches focused attention on the proper role and scope of the federal government, their agendas were very different. These differences contributed to an impasse in budget negotiations that led to a temporary shutdown of the federal government in the fall and winter of 1995-1996.[1] In the wake of this conflict, the NPR shifted focus to highlight its role in reducing the deficit and moving toward a balanced budget as Congress and the Clinton Administration faced the 1996 elections.

---

[1] See U.S. Library of Congress, Congressional Research Service, Shutdown of the Federal Government: Causes, Effects, and Process, by Sharon S. Gressle, CRS Report 98-844 GOV (Washington: Jan. 18, 2001).

THE FIRST NPR STATUS REPORT

In September 1994, Vice President Gore released the first NPR status report, which reviewed the progress that had been made in implementing the 1993 recommendations. Among the claims offered for realizing a government that "works better & costs less" were the following:

- Over 90 percent of National Performance Review recommendations are underway.
- The President has signed 22 directives, as well as performance agreements with seven agency heads.
- Over 100 agencies are publishing customer service standards.
- Nine agencies have started major streamlining initiatives.
- Agencies are forming labor-management partnerships with their unions.
- Agencies are slashing red tape.
- The Government is buying fewer "designed" products and doing more common-sense commercial buying.
- 135 "reinvention laboratories" throughout the federal government are fostering innovation.
- The government is shifting billions of dollars in benefits to electronic payment.
- The federal government is changing the way it interacts with state and local governments.[2]

According to the report, government costs were cut as well.

- $46.9 billion of NPR's $108 billion in proposed savings are already enacted.
- $16 billion in savings is pending before Congress.
- Federal employment has dropped 71,000 positions.
- $695 million in savings results from ending federal subsidies for wool and mohair.
- The Defense Department's overhaul of its travel process will save $1 billion over five years.

---

[2] Office of the Vice President, Creating a Government That Works Better & Costs Less: Status Report. Report of the National Performance Review (Washington: September 1994), p. 5.

- The Federal Communications Commission's auctions of new radio frequencies are raising millions.
- Government's use of a Visa card for small purchases is saving $50 million this year.[3]

The report noted that the executive and legislative branches had cooperated in passing legislation to achieve these results.

- Congress has enacted 21 NPR-related laws, including the first-ever governmentwide "buyout" authority, and mandated cuts in the federal workforce.
- Congress has provided increased flexibility for a variety of programs involving state and local government.
- Congress is about to enact the most significant procurement reform in a decade.
- 47 NPR-related actions passed both houses.
- Another 46 passed one house.
- Congress held more than 80 hearings on various NPR recommendations.[4]

A Brookings Institution report issued at this time also regarded the NPR as having made progress during its first year, with some cautionary caveats. The assessment praised the reform effort's work toward cultural change in the bureaucracy and its success in simplifying some rules and processes, particularly with regard to personnel and procurement, improved coordination of government management through the President's Management Council (PMC), and "widespread innovation by federal managers."[5] At the same time, the report expressed concerns about the sustainability of the NPR reform effort due to four critical problems. First, the NPR sought to change organizational culture at the same time that it was implicitly condemning government employees by criticizing government performance, cutting positions, and challenging entrenched processes. It judged that this two-prong effort was likely to alienate employees, especially those who had weathered previous unsuccessful reforms. Second, the report was concerned that the methods of workforce reduction and other changes overlooked the importance of government capacity. The report's author,

---

[3] Ibid., p. 7.
[4] Ibid., p. 6.
[5] Donald F. Kettl, Reinventing Government? Appraising the National Performance Review, CPS Report 94-2 (Washington: Brookings Institution, 1994), p. 2.

Donald Kettl, wrote of the risk of "an even more hollow government with far less capacity to do its job and managed by employees with even less incentive to do their jobs well."[6] Third, the report expressed concern about the lack of clarity in the core NPR ideas; the principles and purposes behind the reform needed to be more clearly defined or risk losing focus or creating conflicting agendas. Fourth, the reform effort's plan to decentralize government and empower employees to be more entrepreneurial risked damage to accountability, particularly to Congress.

Some in academic circles went beyond the Brookings report in arguing that the entrepreneurial focus of the NPR was in tension with the President's constitutional duty to "take Care that the Laws be faithfully executed."[7] According to these critics, public law creates a system of accountability by the bureaucracy to the President and Congress that is eroded when government functions are decentralized and privatized in the process of establishing entrepreneurial incentives.

The General Accounting Office (GAO) also evaluated the success of the implementation of NPR recommendations on their own terms, assessing progress on each of the 384 major proposals from the September 1993 report as well as the reform effort as a whole. GAO found that about 50% of the recommendations had been fully or partly implemented, noting that the recommendations varied widely in their specificity and scope. It applauded most of the recommendations and achievements of the NPR, but also expressed concern about its failure to address critical management issues that GAO had previously identified. As GAO representatives later testified before the House Subcommittee on Government Management, Information, and Technology in May 1995:

> [The NPR] did not address a number of issues that the Office of Management and Budget and we consider to be high-risk areas. These issues include defense inventory management practices that have resulted in unneeded inventory valued by the Department of Defense at $36 billion and problems plaguing federal information technology initiatives, such as the Federal Aviation Administration's air traffic control modernization project. The NPR recommendations also did not address nearly three-fourths of the issues we identified last year for the former chairman of this Committee as the most important management problems facing 23 federal agencies. These issues include the lack of effective controls over Department of Defense

---

[6] Ibid. p. 3.
[7] U.S. Constitution, Article II, section 3.

disbursements and inadequate project management and planning in the Department of Energy. Therefore, while we believe the recommendations NPR made are an important contribution toward improved federal management, we also believe that significant additional opportunities remain to make government work better and cost less.[8]

Perhaps more significant than the measurement of progress was the GAO call for closer work between Congress and the executive branch on the reforms, greater attention to development and maintenance of agencies' capacities in reform efforts, and more sustained attention to reform by political and career leaders. GAO also urged reformers to refocus evaluation efforts away from "inputs, outputs, and processes to an emphasis on outcomes and results – consistent with the Government Performance and Results Act of 1993."[9] In addition, GAO suggested that the NPR would need a more cohesive statement of its management principles:

> NPR performed a service in highlighting many problems that needed to be addressed and recommending solutions to these problems. However, to be successful in the long run, NPR will need to sharpen its focus and bind the recommendations together into a more coherent framework that can better permit the government reform movement to take root and flourish.[10]

THE NEW REPUBLICAN CONGRESS

Shortly after the NPR's 1994 status report was released, the Republicans won majority control of the House and Senate in mid-term elections, and the focus of the congressional agenda with regard to public administration turned to reducing the size and scope of the federal government. The agenda was based on the Republican's *Contract with America*, which called for "the end of government that is too big, too intrusive, and too easy with the public's money." The new Republican majorities in the House and Senate facilitated passage of the Line Item Veto Act, which President Clinton

---

[8] U.S. General Accounting Office, Government Reform: GAO's Comments on the National Performance Review, GAO testimony, GAO/T-GGD-95-154 (Washington: May 2, 1995), pp. 2-3.
[9] U.S. General Accounting Office, Management Reform: Implementation of the National Performance Review's Recommendations, GAO Report GAO/OCG-95-1 (Washington: Dec. 5, 1994), p. 2.
[10] Ibid., p. 9.

supported and which vested him with more control of unwanted budgetary expenditures.[11] They pressed for passage of the Unfunded Mandates Reform Act of 1995, which limits the ability of the federal government to impose unfounded mandates on state and local governments and requires the provision of information on the costs of federal mandates to the private sector.[12] The Paperwork Reduction Act of 1995 amended the 1980 law of the same name to reduce further the paperwork burden on the public.[13] The Federal Reports Elimination and Sunset Act of 1995 modified or eliminated many federal reporting requirements.[14] The Contract with America Advancement Act of 1996[15] brought two other promises of the *Contract* into law and also raised the public debt limit. Title I reformed Social Security disability programs, while Title II sought to reduce the regulatory burden on small business and improve congressional review of new regulations.

This spate of legislation reflected the difference in focus between the congressional agenda and that of NPR's first phase. While the NPR, in its initial report, had focused on improving government processes, notably customer service and procurement, and on reducing the civilian workforce, the new Republican House majority sought to limit the size and role of the federal government. As one Republican leader was reported to have characterized the difference:

> "The administration's National Performance Review continues to be an important effort," [Representative William F.] Clinger [(R-PA), chairman of the House Government Reform and Oversight Committee,] said: "Improving how our government operates is both necessary and appropriate. But in addition to improving efficiency in government, Republicans believe that we need to limit the ever-expanding size and increasingly intrusive role of the federal government in our lives."[16]

---

[11] 110 Stat. 1200; the statute was subsequently challenged in federal court and ultimately held invalid by the Supreme Court in Clinton v. City of New York, 524 U.S. 417 (1998).
[12] 109 Stat. 48.
[13] 109 Stat. 163.
[14] 109 Stat. 707.
[15] 110 Stat. 847.
[16] Greg Pierce, "Hearings Eye Government Reinvention," Washington Times, May 3, 1995, p. A7.

NPT Enters Phase II

As Republican congressional leaders pursued their agenda, the NPR altered course through a change in emphasis. Without abandoning the 1993 recommendations, the Administration's reform project widened its scope to address the issues the victorious Republicans had raised. In the wake of the congressional elections, President Clinton directed Vice President Gore "to conduct a second review of agencies to identify opportunities for additional savings, program terminations, and privatization of selected functions."[17] In mid-May 1995, OMB Director Alice Rivlin reported to the Senate Committee on Governmental Affairs that Phase II of NPR was shifting the focus of the reform effort from *how* government should operate to *what* it should do, saying:

> The NPR and OMB set up teams to study every function and activity of government to decide which ones the Federal Government should continue to perform, which it should eliminate altogether, and which it should shift to the States, localities, or private sector.[18]

By the time of Rivlin's testimony, related major restructuring either had been announced or was underway in 10 agencies. Although in disagreement about the prescription, by the spring of 1995, both the Clinton Administration and Congress, in their reform discussions, diagnoses, and recommendations, were focused on the proper administrative role of government.

The Administration released its second status report, *Common Sense Government Works Better & Costs Less*, in September 1995.[19] It described progress on the original set of recommendations, and also articulated the administration's new vision for the NPR. Claiming that one third of the original recommendations had been completed and that nearly all of the others were underway, the report also announced more than 180 new recommendations that had arisen for Phase II. As presaged in Rivlin's testimony, the new recommendations focused on devolving, discontinuing, or privatizing government functions.

---

[17] Office of the Vice President, Common Sense Government Works Better & Costs Less: Third Report of the National Performance Review (Washington: September 1995), p. 119.
[18] U.S. Congress, Senate Committee on Governmental Affairs, Executive Branch Reorganization, hearing, 104th Cong., 1st sess., May 17-18, 1995, p. 113.
[19] See citation at note 49.

Despite the similarity of stated government reform goals expressed by Republican congressional leaders and the Administration, wide differences in the scale and location of the reductions were evident in the rhetoric and proposals of each camp. Republican congressional leaders had a bold agenda for decreasing the size of government through contracting out, privatizing government functions, and cutting the number of programs and agencies. For example, Representative John L. Mica (R-FL), chair of the Subcommittee on Civil Service, Committee on Government Reform and Oversight, reportedly proposed contracting out half of the federal government's activities to the private sector.[20] Privatization efforts spearheaded by Representative Scott L. Klug (R-WI) focused on the petroleum reserves, helium reserves, power marketing administrations (PMAs), and the Government Printing Office.[21] Congressional intentions for decreasing the size of the federal government were probably best reflected in the plans of Senate Budget Committee Chairman Pete V. Domenici (R-NM) and House Budget Committee Chairman John Kasich (R-OH), which promised to save $806 billion and $1 trillion, respectively. Both plans called for significant government reductions, Kasich's plan, for example, reportedly called for the elimination of three Cabinet departments, 13 agencies, 68 boards, commissions, and authorities, and over 230 programs.[22]

The savings reported and proposed by the Administration were modest by comparison. The 1995 status report stated that around $58 billion of the originally projected savings of $108 billion had been realized and that the remaining $50 billion was either pending before Congress or "to be acted on in the near future."[23] Some $70 billion in additional savings was projected from the Phase II recommendations. Taken together, these savings were far from the target figures of the congressional Republicans. The federal government reduction envisioned by the NPR also differed from that of the Republicans. Whereas Republican congressional leaders wanted to dismantle entire departments and agencies, recommendations for elimination or revision of regulations by 28 agencies and departments with major

---

[20] Ruth Larson, "More Contracting Sought to Cut Costs," Washington Times, Mar. 30, 1995, p. A8.
[21] Nancy E. Roman, "In GOP's Privatization Drive, Roadblocks Dot Obstacle Course," Washington Times, June 12, 1995, p. A1.
[22] "How to Shrink the Federal Government," Washington Times, May 12, 1995, p. A21; Patrice Hill, "GOP Offers Balanced Budgets: 7-year Plans Cut $1 Trillion," Washington Times, May 10, 1995, p. A1.
[23] Office of the Vice President, Common Sense Government Works Better & Costs Less: Third Report of the National Performance Review, p. 149.

regulatory responsibility formed the focal point of the new phase of the NPR. The NPR report asserted:

- Agencies are sending 16,0-00 pages of obsolete regulations to the scrap heap, of 86,000 pages of regulations reviewed.
- Agencies are reworking another 31,000 pages of regulations.
- Regulatory and administrative burdens on the public will be reduced by nearly $28 billion.
- Attitudes are changing; in many cases, fines will be waived for honest mistakes.
- Agencies are closing more than 2,000 field offices.[24]

According to one observer, Phase II of the NPR was designed to highlight reform work that was underway in the agencies prior to 1995 and the "refocusing" of the NPR was essentially a political response to the results of the midterm elections:

> Increased activity in regulatory reform during 1995 offers a window onto the NPR's methods. Substantive work towards reform was undertaken within the regulatory agencies and not within the task force itself. Those agencies reviewed regulations in the *Code of Federal Regulations* and reassessed and proposed changes in their regulatory procedures. Essentially, at this stage, much of the substantive work of reform was happening in regulatory agencies and was overseen by OMB.[25]

The lack of cooperation between Congress and the executive on government reform had been noted by GAO regarding the 103rd Congress, when the Democrats were in the majority in both Houses of Congress. GAO reiterated this concern regarding the 104th Congress and the Administration in testimony before the Senate Committee on Governmental Affairs, as the following passages illustrate:

> Reorganization demands an integrated approach .... Reorganization plans should be designed to achieve specific, identifiable goals .... Once the goals are identified, the right vehicle(s) must be chosen for accomplishing them ....

---

[24] Ibid., p. 3.
[25] Peri E. Arnold, Making the Managerial Presidency, p. 414.

> Implementation is critical to the success of any reorganization .... Oversight is needed to ensure effective implementation.[26]
>
> The Administration has taken the National Performance Review beyond its initial examination of how government should operate to asking questions about what it should be doing .... In Congress, committees in both Houses have gone farther, mobilizing to study and make far-reaching decisions on the role of government, its basic functions, and organizational structures.[27]
>
> [O]ne cannot underestimate the interconnectedness of government structures and activities. Make changes here, and you will certainly affect something over there. And just as the lack of an overall vision created many of the inefficiencies that exist in the federal government today, reorganization efforts that ignore the broader picture could create new, unintended consequences for the future. For this reason, it is imperative that Congress and the administration form an effective working relationship on restructuring initiatives and regulatory changes.[28]

The Administration's vision of the role of Congress in addressing the proposed NPR reforms was unclear in the 1995 status report. On the one hand, the report continued to credit Congress with support, saying:

- Congress has enacted 36 NPR-related laws, including the biggest procurement streamlining bill ever, with a second in progress.
- Congress has passed 66 of the 280 NPR items requiring legislation (24 percent).
- Nearly 70 NPR-related bills are currently pending in Congress.
- Congress has held more than 120 hearings on various NPR recommendations.[29]

However, on the other hand, the report criticized the Republican majority in Congress for its concept of reducing the size of government.

> [S]ome people, including many in Congress, have decided that the way to fix government is just to eliminate as much of it as

---

[26] U.S. Congress, Senate Committee on Governmental Affairs, Executive Branch Reorganization, p. 103.
[27] Ibid., p. 104.
[28] Ibid., p. 105.
[29] Office of the Vice President, Common Sense Government Works Better & Costs Less: Third Report of the National Performance Review, p. 3.

possible .... The main problem with taking an axe to the federal government is that it won't fix what remains. Government would be smaller, but it would still be as inflexible and bureaucratic.[30]

THE BUDGET IMPASSE

The gulf between the conceptions of government reform and reduction envisioned by Republican congressional leaders and the Clinton Administration contributed to the budget impasses and government shutdown at the beginning of FY1996.[31] Congress proposed legislation that would have made deep cuts in government agencies, in line with the *Contract with America* agenda, while the Administration promoted reductions in government through the efficiencies of reinvention. The NPR was used to articulate the Administration's position during this period, but the Administration's ultimate success did not provide a clear mandate for the future form or scope of government. One analyst observed:

> Despite the rhetorical skirmishes, there was little real sorting out of the government's functions, reorganizing of its operations, or shrinking of its role. In the end the Clinton Administration maneuvered its way out of the crisis by outflanking congressional Republicans. If the administration was politically stronger, however, the reinventing government movement was weakened by the quick shifts in tactics and the diffusion of its focus.[32]

FIRST-TERM NPR

On March 4, 1996, the Vice President consolidated the vision of the NPR to be carried into the 1996 elections. Building on Phase I and II themes in the post budget battle environment, Gore delivered a speech entitled "Governing in a Balanced Budget World." The published documentation accompanying the speech articulated six goals.[33] Most of them, like improving customer service, covered familiar ground. In addition, Gore

---

[30] Ibid., p. 2.
[31] See note 33.
[32] Donald F. Kettl, Reinventing Government: A Fifth-Year Report Card, CPM Report 98-1 (Washington: Brookings Institution, 1998), p. 4.
[33] The speech is available at the archived NPR website, [http://govinfo.library.unt.edu/npr/library/ speeches/272e.html], and the supporting documentation may be found at [http://govinfo.library.unt.edu/npr/library/papers/bkgrd/balbud.html].

advocated the conversion of appropriate agencies to performance-based organizations (PBOs), which would have greater autonomy in their management practices in return for increased accountability to performance standards.

The third status report, which was release later that year, just two months prior to the election, made no mention of PBOs, but rather highlighted NPR themes and summarized the reinvention achievements of the first three years on an agency-by-agency basis. It reported $97.4 billion in savings based on agency implementation of NPR recommendations or their adoption of NPR principles. It also reported personnel reductions, procurement reform, personnel policy reforms, improved customer service, reduced, more streamlined, and less coercive regulation of business, and improved relationships with states and localities.[34]

Assessments of this period of the NPR have varied. One Brookings Institution report suggested that, while reform was sustained within agencies, the central effort waned.[35] Another analysis concluded that, at this point, "the NPR's agenda shifted to fit [reelection] campaign needs."[36] A Heritage Foundation report released in the fall of 1996 compared NPR achievements to "putting new paint on an old termite-infested house with a crumbling foundation," criticizing the reform for missing gross management problems and increasing federal spending even with personnel reductions.[37]

---

[34] Office of the Vice President, The Best Kept Secrets in Government: A Report to President Bill Clinton (Washington: September 1996).
[35] Donald F. Kettl, Reinventing Government: A Fifth-Year Report Card, p. 5.
[36] Peri E. Arnold, Making the Managerial Presidency, p. 415.
[37] Scott A. Hodge, "Reinvention Has Not Ended the 'Era of Big Government'," The Heritage Foundation, Backgrounder 1095 (Washington: Oct. 15, 1996), p. 30.

Chapter 3

NPT RENEWED: PHASE III

In the third and final phase of its reinvention effort, the NPR sought to redefine itself, the goals it sought to accomplish, and the means by which it would do so. This third phase began with the presentation of the *Blair House Papers* to a new Cabinet in 1997 and culminated in the formal change of the NPR's name to the National Partnership for Reinventing Government in 1998. This period was characterized by increasing efforts to involve the American public in government reinvention.

REINVENTING THE REINVENTION EFFORT

In the third phase of its reinvention effort, from 1997-1999, the NPR engaged in three campaigns to further define its agenda and its strategies, as well as reiterate its support for past initiatives. The *Blair House Papers, Businesslike Government: Lessons Learned from America's Best Companies*, and the birth of the National Partnership for Reinventing Government appeared to be attempts to stimulate both public and intragovernmental support for the reinvention cause. However, according to one observer, "the NPR has presented different faces without fundamentally changing its direction, because its overall project of reform has been eclectic from the beginning."[1]

In January 1997, the NPR ushered in its third phase when, as Vice President Gore explained, "President Clinton and I called the new Cabinet to Blair House to give them their reinvention marching orders."[2] The *Blair*

---

[1] Peri E. Arnold, Making the Managerial Presidency, p. 368.
[2] Office of the Vice President, Blair House Papers (Washington: January 1997), p. viii.

House Papers reemphasized traditional NPR rules and principles regarding the delivery of service, the fostering of partnerships and community solutions, and the reinvention of government to "get the job done with less." However, the *Blair House Papers* reiterated and further refined a concept new to the reinventing government debate, the performance-based organization (PBO).

Although the PBO plan was first outlined by Vice President Gore in his March 1996 speech,[3] the model was further refined and placed at the top of the NPR's agency with the *Blair House Papers*. While the PBO is a term of art, is not yet legally defined, and has been used to refer to varying levels of organizational autonomy, the general PBO concept is spelled out in the *Blair House* recommendations.

The PBO model largely relies on business-like practices and is discussed in market terms. It is inspired by the Next Steps Initiative in Great Britain and is based on the idea that organizations, when exempt from federal procurement and personnel rules, will perform more efficiently under new sets of incentives and higher levels of accountability. PBOs are to be managed by a hired chief executive, who will be held accountable to the appropriate department secretary, and this relationship is to be governed by an annual performance agreement. Thus, the chief executive has incentive to ensure that the organization performs well. This is further reinforced by making a portion of the chief executive's salary dependent upon the organization's performance.

Underlying the PBO model is the separation of decision-making and policymaking authority from implementation authority, and candidates for PBO status must fulfill a certain number of prerequisites, which were set out in the *Blair House Papers*.

- Have a clear mission, measurable services, and a performance measurement system in place or in development.
- Generally, focus on external, not internal, customers.
- Have a clear line of accountability to an agency head who has policy accountability for the functions.
- Have top level support to transfer a function into a PBO.
- Have predictable sources of funding.[4]

---

[3] See note 65.
[4] Office of the Vice President, Blair House Papers, p. 42.

Based on these prerequisites, the Clinton Administration identified its first candidates for PBOs in both the *Blair House Papers* and the President's FY1998 budget. They included the National Technical Information Service; the Patent and Trademark Office (PTO); the Seafood Inspection Program of the Department of Commerce; the Defense Commissary Agency; the Saint Lawrence Seaway Development Corporation; the Government National Mortgage Association and the Federal Housing Administration of the Department of Housing and Urban Development; the Federal Retirement and Insurance Service of OPM; and the U.S. Mint.

While the *Blair House Papers* acquainted government leaders with the application of business techniques to governmental problems, the NPR's October 1997 publication, *Businesslike Government: Lessons Learned from America's Best Companies*, sought to do the same for the public. With the help of Scott Adams's "Dilbert" cartoons, the publication demonstrated that business could be a teacher to government as Vice President Gore enlisted the aid of top executives from companies like Disney, Federal Express, and Xerox in the reinvention effort. In the report, Gore reaffirmed the desire to learn from business, noting that American companies "have already been through the transformation from industrial-age to information-age management. They have been through the learning curve, they have made the mistakes and fixed them...."[5] While the report reiterated the basic NPR tenets, it was significant for its efforts to make the NPR and its agenda readily accessible to the American public. In the context of the NPR's evolution, the report reflected the changing nature of the NPR and its outreach beyond the Washington beltway to the general public.

The pinnacle of "reinventing the reinvention effort" was reached in March 1998 when the National Performance Review, on its fifth anniversary, formally became the National Partnership for Reinventing Government. Along with the new name, the NPR adopted new strategies and principles. The NPR no longer sought merely to make government work better and cost less. Instead, it "reorganized into eight teams focused on partnering with federal agencies, state and local governments, the private sector and citizen organizations to:"

- Deliver hassle-free service.
- Create a safer, healthier America.
- Develop stronger and safer communities and families.

---

[5] Office of the Vice President, Businesslike Government: Lessons Learned from America's Best Companies (Washington: October 1997).

- Make the economy stronger.
- Technologically transform America.
- Engage Americans in a conversation about reinventing government.
- Create the most well-managed government in history.
- Model the office of the future.[6]

The NPR sought to achieve these goals by fostering partnerships, encouraging agencies to use "balanced measures," creating an electronic government, and publicizing its message. It focused on 32 "high impact agencies," those with the most interaction with the American people. According to NPR officials, the groups' new plan was to align around a clear vision, value, and goal, and carry on a conversation with Americans about what they value. The NPR would then use results that Americans care about as performance measures. It would partner with "high impact agencies," encourage leadership and pursue fundamental reinvention through people, process and information technology.[7]

Some observers believe the NPR was also perceived as potentially benefiting Vice President Gore's 2000 bid for the presidency. "NPR will be reviewed as if it demonstrates the Vice President's ability to lead, his fiscal understanding of government, can he run a large organization," NPR director Morley Winograd is reported to have commented.[8] From this viewpoint, the NPR attempted to broaden its political appeal by re-focusing its mission.

As the NPR began to commit itself to these broader political goals, the gap between "megapolitics" and front line management began to grow. While Winograd contended that the NPR could create safer neighborhoods by publicizing technological, cultural and process changes made by New York and Boston police,[9] the process reforms that the NPR was undertaking, in the view of one observer, had little or no direct connection with the achievement of the broader goals the NPR had promised the American public.[10] Winograd concluded that, "in seeking political relevance and moving past process, NPR distanced itself from its ability to identify, accomplish and measure results through its own actions."[11] He judged that, in Phase III, the NPR "risked making pledges on which it could not deliver

---

[6] Anne Laurent, "Revamping Reinvention," Government Executive, vol. 30, April 1998, pp0. 31-32.
[7] Ibid.
[8] Ibid., p. 32.
[9] Ibid., p. 34.
[10] Ibid.
[11] Ibid.

and focusing government employees on processes indirectly linked at best with Phase III's broader policy agency."[12]

Although the NPR spent much of 1997-1998 revamping its image and redefining its strategies and goals, government reform efforts continued in other quarters. Overhauling the structure and operations of the Internal Revenue Service (IRS), for example, was a major accomplishment of the 105th Congress. A number of developments contributed to this overhaul. In 1984, the IRS began replacing its outdated computer system. A few years later, GAO questioned the modernization effort and alleged that the IRS had wasted billions of dollars on "unwisely chosen computer purchases" due to the lack of any overall plan for the computer system and a reluctance to engage computer experts outside the IRS. In response, Congress mandated the National Commission on Restructuring the IRS in late 1995.[13] Jaded by Senator Robert Kerrey (D-NE) and Representative Rob Portman (R-OH), the commission sought to evaluate the IRS and make recommendations regarding its organization and practices In November 1997, the panel released its report, *A Vision for a New IRS*, which recommended better congressional oversight of the IRS; a statutorily created independent board of directors to oversee IRS management and operations; a strengthened role for the Secretary of the Treasury in setting tax policy; and expansion of the authority of the IRS commissioner over personnel and senior manager accountability. While legislation advancing the commission's recommendations was introduced with bipartisan support in late July 1997, it was met with strong opposition from the Clinton Administration over the role of the proposed independent board of directors.

Prior to the dissemination of the commission's report, the Administration had announced its intention to reform and reorganize the IRS. Overhaul of the IRS had been one of the original 1993 recommendations made by the NPR. Eventually, a comprehensive plan for IRS reform was unveiled by the Administration in October 1997, with an announcement that it would be implemented immediately. Based on a report by Vice President Gore and Treasury Secretary Robert E. Rubin, the plan focused on improving customer service, giving taxpayers new ways to solve problems, expanding taxpayer rights and remedies, and creating a new IRS board of trustees.[14] However, a few days later, the Clinton Administration abandoned its opposition to congressional reform of the IRS, and legislation

---

[12] Ibid.
[13] 109 Stat. 509.
[14] Al Gore and Robert E. Rubin, "Report on the IRS: Reinvention, Recourse, Rights, Reform," available from [http://www.ustreas.gov/press/releases/prirs1.htm].

embodying the recommendations of the IRS reform commission was subsequently adopted in the House.

In January 1998, the Senate Committee on Finance revealed abuses by the IRS against taxpayers it had accused of non-compliance. These abuses were said to stem from basing performance evaluations of employees on their success in bringing in revenue. The chairman of the Committee on Finance, Senator William V. Roth, Jr. (R-DE), drafted a reform bill and offered it for consideration and markup at a committee meeting on March 31. Roth's bill was adopted in May. A conference report was produced and agreed to by both chambers shortly thereafter, and the measure was signed into law by the President on July 22, 1998.[15]

PERFORMANCE-BASED ORGANIZATIONS

While the NPR and the Clinton Administration identified various candidates for conversion to the PBO model, congressional interest was initially confined to the case of the Patent and Trademark Office (PTO). Congressional attention to the reconstitution of the PTO as a PBO began early in 1995, and the 104th Congress subsequently saw an Administration proposal, three House bills, and two Senate bills on the matter offered for consideration. All of these measures, even those converting the PTO into a government corporation, embraced basic PBO concepts of "marketizing" governmental functions in order to improve the delivery of services.[16] However, none of them received final legislative approval, and the issue of PTO conversion continued into the 105th Congress, when two omnibus bills and an additional Senate proposal were introduced. Again, the proposed measures were not passed by Congress, and the Administration indicated that legislation converting the PTO to PBO status would be offered in the 105th Congress (see H.R. 1907).

In many regards, converting the PTO to PBO status did not succeed because the NPR seemingly failed to anticipate congressional, union, and intragovernmental unwillingness to increase the autonomy of the PTO by

---

[15] 112 Stat. 685.
[16] Government corporations are federal agencies established by Congress to serve a public purpose by performing a market-oriented service which produces enough revenue to meet or approximate the expenditures of the corporation. They share a number of characteristics with PBS, such as the "marketization" of activities and the application of business practices to governmental functions. See U.S. Library of Congress, Congressional Research Service, Federal Government Corporations: An Overview, by Ronald C. Moe, CRS Report RL30365 (Washington: Nov. 1, 2000).

making it a PBO. Without an effective strategy for dealing with Congress, the NPR had relied on administrative action to accomplish many of its goals. However, the conversion of the PTO to PBO status could occur only through legislative action, and there was a considerable amount of congressional resistance to relinquishing control over agencies as "[t]he PBO concept would place more power in the hands of the few, [and] Congress would lose some of its oversight authority."[17] Furthermore, labor unions strongly opposed a PBO conversion that would exempt the PTO from existing personnel rules. In addition, some saw executive branch resistance to PBO conversion legislation freeing the PTO from the General Services Administration's monopoly on real property services, which the Administration's bill did not do.[18]

The first PBO was created with the enactment of the Higher Education Amendments of 1998 when the Department of Education's student financial services were vested in a new Office of Student Financial Assistance (OSFA).[19] Headed by a chief operating officer selected by the Secretary of Education, the OSFA was given independent control of its budget and finances, personnel decisions and processes, procurements, and other administrative and management functions. Compensation of the chief operating officer was based partially upon organizational performance. In return for this independence, the OSFA must improve student services, reduce costs, and increase the accountability of administration. The office's performance is measured in accordance with a five-year plan, developed by the Secretary of Education and the chief operating officer of the OSFA, that establishes measurable goals and objectives for the organization. Furthermore, oversight of the organization is performed through the Secretary, who maintains authority to direct the PBO in the implementation of its functions.

The OSFA example highlights the difficulties that the NPR had in converting government agencies into PBOs. While the Administration had long sought to convince Congress to convert the PTO and Saint Lawrence Seaway Development Corporation to PBO status, the Department of Education proposal was easily accepted. In the House, the Higher Education Amendments of 1998 were adopted on a 414-4 vote, and in the Senate, they

---

[17] U.S. Congress, House Committee on Government Reform and Oversight, Oversight of Performance-Based Organizations, hearing, 105th Cong., 1st sess., July 8, 1997 (Washington: GPO, 1998), p. 5.

[18] Alasdair Roberts, "Performance Based Organizations: Assessing the Gore Plan," Public Administration Review, vol. 57, November-December 1997, p. 470.

[19] 112 Stat. 1581, at 1604; see Brian Friel, "Congress Creates Performance-Based Organization,:" available at [http://www.govexec.com/dailyfed/0798/071498b1.htm].

were approved on a 96-1 vote. Subsequently, the conference report was passed by the House on a voice vote and by the Senate on a 96-0 recorded vote. The ease of passage may be attributed to the genesis of this particular initiative. Although the PBO model had been developed and promoted by the Administration, the initiative for the creation of OSFA came from the Republicans on the House Committee on Education and the Workforce, which adapted the Administration's idea and applied it to the financial aid services.

The creation of the first PBO revitalized Administration efforts to reinvent government by marketizing governmental functions. In February 1999, the President's FY2000 budget indicated that the PTO, Defense Commissary Agency, U.S. Mint, and Seafood Inspection Service, which had been proposed for conversion to PBO status in past years, would be offered again as PBO candidates in the 106th Congress. Other entities recommended for PBO status were the Rural Telephone Bank, the National Technical Information Service, and the Federal Lands Highway Program. Late in 1999, the President signed a consolidated appropriations bill that included the American Inventors Protection Act, which reorganized the PTO as an independent agency within the Department of Commerce, but, contrary to the claim of the reconstituted PTO, did not transform it, in the view of many analysts, into a PBO.[20]

In the closing weeks of his tenure, President Clinton, with E.O. 13180 of December 7, 2000, directed the Secretary of Transportation, consistent with his legal authorities, to establish a PBO – to be known as the Air Traffic Organization (ATO) – within the Federal Aviation Administration (FAA).[21] He had recommended the establishment of such an entity to Congress in 1997 and, more recently, in his FY2001 budget, but legislators had shown little interest in the proposal. Intended to produce more efficient management of air traffic services at a time when airline delays and cancellations were mounting, the new ATO would count some 37,000 FAA employees engaged in air traffic control, air traffic facilities maintenance and repair, and selected research and acquisitions activities. However, the statutorily mandated Chief Operating Office of the current Air Traffic Control System was to head the ATO, a feature differing from the PBO model advanced by the NPR in 1996.

There were indications in May 2001 that the successor Bush Administration was interested in converting the Department of State's

---

[20] See 113 Stat. 1537-574.
[21] See Federal Register, vol. 65, Dec. 11, 2000, pp. 77493-77494.

Foreign Buildings Operation, which serves as the landlord for U.S. facilities overseas, into a PBO.

THE REPORT CARDS AND BEYOND

In a late 1998 website bulletin, NPR staff summarized the organization's 1993-1998 accomplishments. Coupling this summary with the NPR's agenda suggests that the NPR measures succeeded in a number of ways. Included as indicators of success were cost savings, decreased "red tape" and regulations, downsizing, the use of reinvention principles by federal employees, and the creation of laws based on NPR recommendations. The summary proffered the following major accomplishments of the NPR.

- Savings total[ing] $137 billion.
- Federal agencies have published more than 4,000 customer service standards for more than 570 organizations and programs.
- Agencies have eliminated more than 16,000 pages of regulations. President Clinton signed an Executive Order requiring rules and other public documents to be written in plain language.
- Government was reduced by 351,000 positions. Reductions occurred in 13 of 14 departments. (Justice increased crime fighting.)
- More than 12,000 Hammer Awards have been presented to teams of federal workers and their partner sin industry and state and local governments for using reinvention principles to create a government that works better, costs less, and delivers results Americans care about.
- About 340 reinvention labs are reengineering government processes and using technology to unleash innovations that excite customers and employees alike with more flexible internal systems and improved services to the public.
- The Congress has passed and President Clinton has signed more than 83 laws so far enacting NPR recommendations.[22]

---

[22] National Partnership for Reinventing Government, Summary of Accomplishments, 1993-1998; modified and updated version available at [http://govinfo.library.unt.edu/npr/whoweare/appendixf.html].

These indicators and measures of success, however, were not accepted in some quarters. For example, in a July 1999 report, the GAO questioned the amount of savings claimed by the NPR, saying:

> NPR claimed savings from agency-specific recommendations that could not be fully attributed to its efforts. In general, the savings estimates we reviewed could not be replicated, and there was no way to substantiate the savings claimed. We also found that some savings were overstated because OMB counted savings twice, and two of the estimates were reported incorrectly, resulting in claims that were understated.[23]

The NPR was concerned with downsizing as a way to combat "big government" and to make government work better and cost less. However, one seasoned observer states, these downsizing efforts proved detrimental to morale among government employees and failed to win political favor with the American public.[24] This downsizing produced larger cuts in the front-line government employees than in the middle levels of federal government. This development was contrary to the Administration's promise to cut middle management, who "pushed paper and contributed to the bureaucracy," and to preserve the top managers, who made decisions, and the front-line employees, who delivered the services.[25]

This observer, Donald Kettl, gave the NPR and its government reinvention efforts a favorable review and an overall grade of B. He acknowledged that the NPR had forged new ground, sustained the reinvention effort, and realized important accomplishments. Among these, he gave procurement reform an A and the NPR an A+ for effort. However, he gave the NPR a D for identifying the objectives of government and for relations with Congress. Incomplete grades were assigned for improving results in "high impact" programs and for service coordination.[26]

While Kettl delivered a favorable, yet critical, review of the NPR, he brought to light important challenges that the organization would have to grapple with in order to continue reinvention efforts in the remaining months of the Clinton Administration. He indicated that perhaps the greatest challenge to the NPR's efforts had been a guarded and, sometimes, resistant Congress.

---

[23] U.S. General Accounting Office, NPR's Savings: Claimed Agency Savings Cannot All Be Attributed to NPR, GAO Report GAO/GGD-99-120 (Washington: July 1999), p. 13.
[24] See Donald F. Kettl, Reinventing Government: A Fifth Year Report Card, pp. 5, 34.
[25] See Ibid., pp. 19-20.
[26] See Ibid., p. ix.

> [T]he NPR's strategy of integrating government services conflicted with Congress's traditional – and fragmented – committee jurisdictions. For the NPR's first 18 months, a not always friendly Democratic Congress saw little reason to tangle with management reform while fighting battles on health care and other Clinton proposals. For the next three years, a Republican Congress has no interest in acting on initiatives put forward by the leading candidate for the Democratic party's 2000 presidential nomination.[27]

However, Congress has not been the only entity to challenge NPR reinvention efforts. Resistance also exists within the executive branch. Kettl further found that the NPR failed to enlist support for reinvention from the Administration's own political appointees and from senior career civil servants. This failure, he noted, produced an NPR campaign with uneven effects among the agencies, particularly where appointed leaders failed to connect with the reinvention effort.[28] Moreover, executive branch concerns about deregulation and PBOs have delayed the implementation of the Administration's PBO plan. "The delay," according to one observer, "is largely attributable to difficulties in resolving about he legislative freedoms that ought to be given to these organizations."[29] This has been exacerbated by the ambivalence of central management agencies and the reluctance of parent departments to give greater autonomy and flexibility to their agencies.

---

[27] Ibid., p. 34.
[28] Ibid.
[29] Alasdair Roberts, "Performance Based Organizations: Assessing the Gore Plan," p. 470.

Chapter 4

SUCCESSES, PROBLEMS, AND REMAINING QUESTIONS

Just before the NPR began its final year of activities and operations, it crafted. In late 1998, a two-year strategy designed to "forever change" government through five initiatives.

- Achieve outcomes no one agency can achieve along.
- Agencies use a balanced set of measures.
- Create an electronic government.
- Transform agencies with the greatest impact on Americans.
- Mobilize America's real heroes to get the message out.[1]

Although the realization of this plan required more time than would be available to the NPR, what may be said, in the aftermath of the NPR experience, about its legacy – successes, problems, and remaining questions?

SUCCESSES

Concerning successes, Peri E. Arnold, a veteran analyst of federal reorganization and reform efforts, has suggested that the NPR be considered in terms of the implementation of its specific recommendations, the

---

[1] John Kamensky, "A Brief History," National Partnership for Reinventing Government (Washington: January 1999), pp. 6-9, available at [http://govinfo.library.unt.edu/npr/whoweare/historyofnpr.html]; Bill Landauer, "Gore's NPR Must Reform Itself to Survive," Federal Times, Sept. 6, 1999, p. 5.

instillation of "a new culture of administration within the executive branch," and the creation of "a centrist coalition to support" the leadership of "a pragmatic Democratic president."[2]

Reviewing the record concerning the implementation of NPR recommendations, Arnold offered the following summary of the situation.

> In reports issued in December 1994 and again in June 1996, the GAO tracked adoption of the NPR's September 1993 recommendations. The 1994 GAO assessment of the adoption of the September 1993 NPR recommendations found that there had been some implementation action taken on 93 percent of those recommendations; of these 4 percent had been fully implemented, 37 percent had been partially implemented, and 50 percent had begun implementation. Another 2 percent had been acted upon in a way consistent with the recommendations' purposes, 2 percent could not be assessed given limited information, and only 5 percent of the recommendations had seen no action at all. In a 1996 study the GAO confined examination to just those recommendations for which adoption had been claimed in the September 1995 *Common Sense Government* [report]. That second annual NPR progress report claimed that a third of its recommended actions had been completed. The GAO's report demurred, finding that 24 percent of the recommendations had been fully implemented (and with most others still in progress, as had been reported by the GAO in 1994). Thus, in one year the rate of completion of recommendations had grown from 4 percent to 24 percent, and there seemed general support for action on many of the remaining recommendations.[3]

To this record of implementation or partial implementation of many NPR recommendations may be added some other concrete achievements. For example, as Arnold noted, while agency action accounted for the implementation of at least 292 recommendations, the NPR was not completely lacking in legislative success.

---

[2] Peri E. Arnold, Making the Managerial Presidency, p. 419.
[3] Ibid., pp;. 419-420; the GAO reports mentioned are U.S. General Accounting Office, Management Reform: Implementation of the National Performance Review's Recommendations, GAO Report GAO/OCG-95-1 (Washington: December 1994); U.S. General Accounting Office, Management Reform: Completion Status of Agency Actions Under the National Performance Review, GAO Report GAO/GGD-96-94 (Washington: June 1996).

> Legislative action was the second most common means of implementation [of NPR recommendations]. By December 1994, 169 of the recommendations were introduced within legislation and 83 recommendations were enacted. Presidential actions addressed at least 86 recommendations. Also, congressional support for reinvention continued into the Republican Congress after 1994. There was a substantial synergy between the new Republican agenda for reducing government and the NPR's recommendations for simplifying government. Thus legislation such as the Unfunded Mandate Reform Act of 1995, the Small Business Lending Enhancement Act of 1995, and several of the 1996 appropriations acts incorporated NPR recommendations.[4]

The NPR later reported that, as of March 1998, for those recommendations requiring presidential or congressional action, "President Clinton signed 46 directives and Congress passed and the President signed over 85 laws."[5]

Another accomplishment proffered by the NPR: cutting the federal workforce by 351,000 positions, making it "the smallest since Kennedy held office and, as a percentage of the national workforce, the smallest since 1931."[6] Donald Kettl noted that "careful analysis of the long-term employment trends shows that downsizing in the Pentagon began *before* the NPR's launch," and "cynics contended that the NPR simply ratified reductions in the Defense Department's civilian workforce that were going to occur anyway." Nonetheless, he concluded that, "if the NPR accomplished nothing else, it certainly produced a substantial and sustained reduction in federal employment – virtually across the board – in a way never before seen in the federal government."[7]

One other achievement that the NPR reported was the elimination of some 640,000 pages of internal agency rules and about 16,000 pages of federal regulations, with another 31,000 pages being rewritten in plain language.[8]

Additionally, the NPR claimed cost savings totaling about $137 billion as a result of its efforts, although that figure was recently contested by GAO. Nonetheless, Kettl advised:

---

[4] Peri E. Arnold, Making the Managerial Presidency, pp. 421-422.
[5] John Kamensky, "A Brief History," p. 5.
[6] Ibid.
[7] Donald F. Kettl, Reinventing Government: A Fifth-Year Report Card, p. 18 (emphasis in original).
[8] John Kamensky, "A Brief History," p. 5.

> While the NPR unquestionably produced cost savings, especially in procurement and reduction in government employment, assessing which of the NPR's recommendations produced how much savings is a virtually impossible job. In part, this is because it usually proved difficult to predict what costs would have been without the NPR. In part, this is because the government's cost account systems frequently make such analyses impossible.[9]

Another consideration offered by Arnold regarding the success of the NPR concerned the instillation of "a new culture of administration within the executive branch." Arnold commented:

> Predecessor comprehensive reform efforts have been static. They attempted a wave of reforms at a point in time, aiming at enhancing presidential managerial capacities and streamlining federal administrative structure and processes. In contrast, the NPR seeks to be dynamic. To the degree that anything unites its recommendations, the NPR's advocates understand its reforms as creating a changed economy of incentives within federal administration such that individuals will be motivated to be creative about the way they work, more productive in their work, and more responsible for the success of their organization. In the vocabulary of reinvention, the attitudes consistent with reinvention's economy of incentives would constitute a new administrative culture.[10]

Concrete achievements claimed in this area include the honoring of over 1,200 federal innovation teams with the Vice President's Hammer Award and the creation of over 350 Reinvention Labs to test ways that agencies could improve their performance and customer service by reengineering work processes and eliminating unnecessary regulations.[11] Reporting on the Reinvention Labs in March 1996, the GAO indicated that "the labs' results suggest a number of promising approaches to improving existing agency work processes," but noted that "the real value of the labs will be realized only when the operational improvements they initiated, tested, and validated achieved wider adoption."[12]

---

[9] Donald F. Kettl, Reinventing Government: A Fifth-Year Report Card, p. 22.
[10] Peri E. Arnold, Making the Managerial Presidency, p. 423.
[11] John Kamensky, "A Brief History," p. 5.
[12] U.S. General Accounting Office, Management Reform: Status of Agency Reinvention Lab Efforts, GAO Report GAO/GGD-96-69 (Washington: March 1996), p. 3.

Another success cited was the commitment of over 570 federal organization to more than 4,000 customer service standards.[13]

Finally, regarding Arnold's third consideration, how successful had the NPR been in creating "a centrist coalition to support" the leadership of President Clinton? Arnold commented:

> Bill Clinton initiated the NPR to address a governing context that was substantially different from that in which presidents had earlier used administrative reform to construct the managerial presidency. The emergent context of the late 20th century is fragmented and characterized by weak parties, mercurial interest groupings, weakened public institutions, and a technology allowing intense and pervasive public focus on presidents. Like Carter and Reagan before him, Clinton sought to use administrative reform in this emerging context to respond to public hostility toward government.[14]

Perhaps the NPR bespeaks success in this regard when reporting:

> Most importantly, public trust in the federal government is finally increasing after a 30-year decline. Various polls have shown a clear and steady increase over the past four years. While it is not clear this is directly linked to the results of reinvention, we believe reinvention has made an important contribution.[15]

Arnold, however, appeared to be more certain about this area of success, and concluded:

> The reinvention of government has been a side show in some respects. After all, administrative reform is "a second-level issue" in presidential politics. However, reinvention is an enterprise that reflects well upon Clinton and Gore. It reinforces their own optimal self-descriptions and gives testimony that these leaders are addressing the problems that trouble most Americans.[16]

In September 2000, a GAO report concluded that the NPR reinvention effort had been largely successful, with more than 90% of key Clinton Administration recommendations having been fully or partly implemented.

---

[13] John Kamensky, "A Brief History," p. 5.
[14] Peri E. Arnold, Making the Managerial Presidency, p. 433.
[15] John Kamensky, "A Brief History," p. 5.
[16] Peri E. Arnold, Making the Managerial Presidency, p. 434.

The report was based upon a review of 72 NPR recommendations by 10 federal agencies, and found that 33 of them were fully implemented and another 30 were partly implemented.[17]

PROBLEMS

Some of the problems encountered by the NPR were noted previously and those identified here should not be regarded as constituting an exhaustive list.

Although the NPR enjoyed some cooperation from Congress, as the legislative record of NPR recommendations legislated into law indicates, the NPR does not appear to have had a clear strategy for working with Congress. Most NPR recommendations seem to have been implemented through a strategy of agency acceptance and presidential orders. The overall record, Arnold observed, reflects "Congress's support for individual items" among the NPR recommendations "and its disinterest in the NPR's conception of reinvention."[18] Agreeing with this assessment, Kettl concluded:

> Efforts to develop legislative support for NPR initiatives have, with the exception of procurement reform, been weak and ineffective. Support from Congress: poor.[19]

The NPR's efforts sometimes resulted in a loss of morale among federal civil servants. Part of reason for this problem, as Kettl noted, was the tension between the NPR's emphasis, on the one hand, on downsizing and reengineering and, on the other hand, customer service.

> A flatter organization, driven by customer service, demands energetic and highly motivated employees. A cost-cutting, reengineered and downsized operation often discourages employees. Trying to do both risks putting the basic incentives at cross purposes; focusing on either risks leaving the corporation stuck in old-style, less productive approaches. The NPR took in the competing ideas without fundamentally sorting them out.[20]

---

[17] U.S. General Accounting Office, Reinventing Government: Status of NPR Recommendations at 10 Federal Agencies, GAO Report GAO/GGD-00-145 (Washington: September 2000).
[18] Peri E. Arnold, Making the Managerial Presidency, p. 422.
[19] Donald F. Kettl, Reinventing Government: A Fifth-Year Report Card, p. ix.
[20] Ibid., p. 9.

Coupling morale deflation with agency leadership in support of NPR reinvention efforts, Kettl offered the following scenario.

> In a 1996 survey conducted by the Merit Systems Protection Board, only 37 percent of federal employees believed that their organization had made reinvention a top priority. The NPR's management improvement goals penetrated far less into the Pentagon than in civilian agencies. Morale in many agencies was poor. Only 20 percent of federal workers said that the NPR had brought positive change to government. This response, however, varied directly with how much workers believed that their agencies' officials had made the NPR's goals a top agency priority. Where the NPR was a top priority, 59 percent of employees thought productivity had improved; where it was not, just 32 percent saw productivity improvements. The lesson: where agency managers promoted the NPR's goals, employees were three times more likely to think that government organizations had made good use of their abilities. They were almost twice as likely to believe that they had been given greater flexibility. The NPR succeeded in motivating employees, quite predictably, to the degree to which top government officials made this an important goal. Where they did not – and the survey suggests that the NPR deeply penetrated only about a third of all federal agencies – the NPR became known principally for its downsizing focus and consequently motivation lagged.[21]

Kettl also suggested that the NPR had a public confidence problem, including both outreach or visibility and credibility.

> A June 1998 Scripps Howard News Service survey showed that citizens tended not to believe that the NPR had accomplished what it claimed. Although 54 percent of those surveyed said that they had heard of reinventing government, 59 percent did not believe that the administration had in fact reduced the number of federal employees as the NPR claimed, even though those claims were fully accurate. More respondents – 61 percent – did not believe that the federal government had become more efficient, even though there is a strong case for substantial improvements. Coupled with the Republicans' takeover of Congress in 1994 and the NPR's constant problems in gaining political traction for its

---

[21] Ibid., p. 17.

message, reinventing government ran headlong into tough confidence problems indeed.[22]

The NPR also had a problem framing its approach to, and focus on, reform. The NPR effort lacked a theoretical base and cohesion among its broad range of ideas. The NPR largely devoted its attention to the process of government rather than the more basic questions of what government should do, which many experts believe should come first. James D. Carroll, a public administration expert, observed:

> In defining government as an appendage of the economy, the NPR strips the federal government of what is distinctively governmental – ultimately enforcement of binding norms through legitimate coercion to maintain a legal, normative order. In treating government as a Wal-Mart, the NPR ignores the fact that many operational assumptions based on customer service have implications for broader systems of values such as the rule of law, representative government, separated and shared powers, and individual liberty.[23]

Carroll also observed that the NPR gave no attention to the constitutional basis of American national government or its significance for administration. Ultimately, he concluded, these theoretical shortcomings resulted in some critical myopia in the NPR reform effort.

> Neither phase [I or II] of the NPR directly and systematically addresses trends that probably will shape much of public administration in the early 21st century. The first is the imbalance between consumption and savings and investment in the United States marked by concern with deficits and debt, entitlement spending, demographic change, and declining private and public investment. The second is the challenge of sorting out relationships and responsibilities among levels of government, and governments and other organizations. The third is reconciling traditions of constitutional governance and legal accountability with the search for flexibility, innovation, and productivity in addressing managerial and programmatic issues.[24]

---

[22] Ibid., p. 36.
[23] James D. Carroll, "The Rhetoric of Reform and Political Reality in the National Performance Review," Public Administration Review, vol. 55, May-June 1995, p. 310.
[24] Ibid., p. 302.

Kettl found there was a compounding effect to some of the NPR's shortcomings.

> NPR is most notable for its failure to grapple with ... basic organizational issues. It reduced the number of supervisors without transforming federal management practice. Its top officials preached the virtues of reducing middle management just as the private sector was rediscovering the importance of middle managers as "high-impact players." The NPR failed to deal with the layering of government and, especially, with the 3,000 political appointees that encrust the top of the federal bureaucracy – for the obvious political reasons. That failure, coupled with its failure to enlist those appointees aggressively in its cause, marked a major shortcoming of the NPR. It also made it harder for the NPR to deliver on its promise to downsize middle-level management en route to better customer service. It is hard to reduce the distance from top managers to the shop floor when the shop floor – those who actually deliver the government's goods and services – increasingly lies outside the government [as a consequence of contracting out].[25]

Finally, in addition to prompting a downsizing of frontline federal employees, not middle managers, and otherwise lowering the morale of many civil servants,[26] the NPR, Carroll noted, did "not propose a systematic agenda for rebuilding the career service," and its "overall message ... on the career service is ambivalent or negative."[27]

REMAINING QUESTIONS

Two of Carroll's comments concerning problems NPR engendered in its reinvention effort suggest some matters that may continue to draw policymakers' attention. The first of these involves addressing trends likely to shape much of public debate in the early part of the 21st century – the imbalance between consumption and savings and investment in the United States, entitlement spending, demographic change, and declining private and public investment; sorting out relationships and responsibilities among different levels of government as well as governments and other

---

[25] Donald F. Kettl, Reinventing Government: A Fifth-Year Report Card, pp. 21-22.
[26] See Ibid., pp. 19-20.
[27] James D. Carroll, "The Rhetoric of Reform and Political Reality in the National Performance Review," p. 309.

organizations; and reconciling traditions of constitutional governance and legal accountability with realizing flexibility, innovation, and productivity in addressing managerial and programmatic issues.

A second question concerns the need for a systematic agenda for rebuilding the career civil service and pursuing that agenda to establish new policy. Addressing this question at the end of 1999, James D. Carroll, noting that the NPR "postponed the examination of some fundamental realities that future efforts to improve federal management will have to address, suggested three items for the 21st century management reform agenda. The first of these derived from "the decline of the traditional administrative state and the rise of the entitlement state." Carroll commented:

> In fiscal year 1962, 63 percent of federal spending was discretionary in that it was appropriated on an annual basis in response to the President's budget proposal. In fiscal year 2000, only 33 percent of spending is discretionary. The remainder is legally committed under entitlement, debt instrument, or other devices.
> The administrative state of the 1930s and thereafter was based on a problem-solving model of public management. In this model, in response to constituent and interest group pressures, politicians defined problems in legislative form. They then assigned the problems to agencies. The agencies' managers and technicians then exercised their skill, judgment, professionalism, and discretion in planning, budgeting, and otherwise defining and acting upon a problem. In the entitlement state, the President and Congress establish program structures that constrain managerial discretion as well as future legislative direction. Budgeting rules, particularly the Budget Enforcement Acts, have reinforced the emergence of these algorithmic structures and processes. The challenge for the next agenda for public management is to determine how the entitlement state can be configures to allow the exercise of managerial judgment and skills.[28]

A second item derived from "the emergence of Congress as a co-manager of the administrative branch," including government corporations and regulatory commissions. In Carroll's view, factors strengthening congressional influence over administration included "the program structures and other provisions of the entitlement state"; the congressional role in the budget process; and "the aggressiveness of Congress in establishing a new,

---

[28] James D. Carroll, "An Agenda for Reforming Federal Management in the 21st Century," The Business of Government, Fall 1999, pp. 16-17.

although somewhat fragmented, framework for federal management in the 1990s," with such laws as the Chief Financial Officers Act, the Government Performance and Results Act, and the Federal Financial Management Improvement Act, among others. The resulting agenda item was "for the executive and Congress to sort out who is responsible for what in agency and program management."[29]

A third item Carroll cited arises from changes in constitutional law. "Federal managers," he said, "increasingly must understand the Supreme Court's actions in order to act effectively and legally." Among these actions, the Court has held that "privatization and related forms of the new public management are subject to constitutional scrutiny"; "launched a fundamental re-examination of the distribution of powers in the federal system, focused on questions of the limitations of the federal government's powers"; and "continued to hold individual public administrators liable in money damages for their failure to consider the constitutional implications of their actions under federal civil rights legislation and other provisions of law." Consequently, the item for the federal management reform agenda is "to develop new public management frameworks that enable public managers to function effectively in this new constitutional framework."[30]

In testimony offered at a May 4, 2000, Senate Governmental Affairs subcommittee hearing on reinventing government, a GAO representative identified six "of the more important management problems that will confront the next Congress and administration" in the period after the NPR effort:

- Adopting an effective results orientation,
- Coordinating crosscutting programs,
- Addressing high-risk federal functions and programs,
- Developing and implementing modern human capital practices,
- Strengthening financial management, and
- Enhancing computer security.[31]

Reinvention downsizing of the federal workforce was seen as resulting in a problematic legacy. According to the GAO witness:

---

[29] Ibid., p. 17.
[30] Ibid.
[31] U.S. Congress, Senate Committee on Governmental Affairs, Has Government Been "Reinvented"?, hearing, 106th Cong., 2nd sess., May 4, 2000 (Washington: GPO, 2000), p. 34.

> The manner in which the downsizing was implemented has short- and long-term implications that require continuing attention. The management control positions NPR sought to decrease were barely reduced as a proportion of the workforce as a whole, and at some agencies they increased.
>
> In addition, our reviews have found that a lack of adequate strategic and workforce planning during the initial rounds of downsizing by some agencies may have affected their ability to achieve organizational missions. Some agencies reported that downsizing in general led to such negative effects as a loss of institutional memory and an increase in work backlogs. ...
>
> Although we found that agencies' planning for downsizing improved as their downsizing efforts continued, it is by no means clear that the current workforce is adequately balanced to properly execute agencies' missions today.[32]

Continued improvements in acquisitions management were thought to be needed.

> Reform efforts, including the Federal Acquisition Streamlining Act of 1994 and the Clinger-Cohen Act of 1996, have focused principally on simplifying the process for buying commercial products and services and on attempting to improve decision-making in acquiring information technology.
>
> Despite these reforms, however, the products and services the government buys all too often cost more than expected, are delivered late, or fail to perform as anticipated. No commercial business would remain viable for very long with results like these. Problems are particularly evident in the two areas where most of the dollars are spent – on weapons systems and information technology. Significant improvements in these areas, as well as in the skills of the acquisition workforce, are needed in order to produce better outcomes.[33]

Finally, it was also thought that the NPR's initiatives to improve the federal regulatory system by streamlining agency rulemaking and cutting regulations had, at best, "yielded mixed results."[34]

By implication, the comment by the GAO witness that prevailing management problems "continue to demand attention: poses the question of a successor to the NPR. Options include another temporary task force like

---

[32] Ibid., pp. 40-41.
[33] Ibid., p. 42.
[34] Ibid., p. 43.

the NPR, a temporary national study commission on government reform, a designated unit in an existing agency (*e.g.*, OMB, GAO), or the creation of a new agency, such as an Office of Management, perhaps vested with some of the management responsibilities currently assigned to OMB.

CLOSURE

The NPR continued operations until the final day of the Clinton Administration, January 19, 2001. Documents available from the NPR Web site as of that closing date were subsequently made available via the Internet through a Web site jointly created and maintained by the Government Printing Office and the University of North Texas Libraries to facilitate continued access to this electronic archival repository ([http://govinfo.library.unt.edu/npr/default.html]).

INDEX

A

accountability, 12, 20, 22, 25, 27, 40, 42
administrative action, 27
Air Traffic Control System, 28
air traffic control, 12, 28
Air Traffic Organization (ATO), 28
Alaska Power Administration, 5
American Inventors Protection Act, 28
American public, 21, 23, 24, 30
Americans, 24, 29, 33, 37
annual performance agreement, 22

B

balanced budget, 9
Blair House Papers, 21-23
budget and finances, 27
Budget Enforcement Acts, 42
budget negotiations, 9
budgetary expenditures, 14
budgeting, 2, 42
bureaucracy, x, 1, 11, 12, 30, 41

C

Carter, President, 37
citizens, x, 1, 4, 39
civil service, 42
civilian workforce, 14, 35
Clinger-Cohen Act, 44
Clinton Administration, viii, 9, 15, 19, 23, 25, 26, 30, 37, 45
Clinton, President Bill, x, xi, 1, 3, 5-7, 13, 15, 20, 21, 28, 29, 35, 37
Committee on Finance, 26
Committee on Governmental Affairs, 6, 15, 17, 18, 43
Committees on Appropriations, 5
Common Sense Government, 15, 16, 18, 34
Community Enterprise Board, 5
competition, 3
computer security, 43
conflicting agendas, 12
Congressional Budget Office (CBO), ix, x
congressional elections, vii, 15
congressional Republicans, 16, 19
constitutional governance, 40, 42
constitutional law, 43
Contract with America Advancement Act, 14
Contract with America, vii, 9, 13, 19
contracting out, 16, 41
cost savings, 29, 35, 36
crop insurance reform bill, 6

Index

customer satisfaction, 3
customer service standards, 10, 29, 37
customer service, 10, 14, 20, 25, 29, 36-38, 40, 41

D

debt, 40, 42
decentralization, 3
Defense Commissary Agency, 23, 28
Defense Department, 2, 10, 35
deficits, 40
Democratic Congress, 31
Democrats, 17
demographic change, 40, 41
Department of Agriculture, 5, 6
Department of Commerce, 28
Department of Defense, 12
Department of Education, 27
Department of Energy, 13
Department of Housing and Urban Development, 5, 23
directives, vii, 6, 10, 35
downsizing efforts, 30, 44
downsizing, vii, ix, 4, 7, 29, 30, 35, 38, 39, 41, 44

E

economy, 3, 24, 36, 40
electronic government, 24, 33
empowerment zones, 5
enterprise communities, 5
entitlement spending, 40, 41
entitlement, 1, 40- 42
entrepreneurial government, x, 3
environment, 2, 19
executive branch, 3, 9, 13, 27, 31, 34, 36

F

Federal Acquisition Streamlining Act, 6, 44
federal administrative structure, 36
Federal Aviation Administration (FAA), 12, 28
federal civil rights legislation, 43
Federal Communications Commission, 11
federal employees, 1, 29, 39, 41
Federal Financial Management Improvement Act, 43
Federal Government, ix, 1, 9, 15, 16, 26
Federal Lands Highway Program, 28
Federal Reports Elimination and Sunset Act, 14
federal spending, 20, 42
federal subsidies, 10
federal workers, 29, 39
Federal Workforce Restructuring Act, 6
financial management, 2, 43

G

General Accounting Office (GAO), ix, x, 12, 13, 17, 25, 30, 34-38, 43-45
General Government Appropriations Act, 5
General Services Administration, 2, 27
Gingrich, Speaker Newt, 9
Gore, Jr., Vice President Albert, vii, x, 1, 2, 5, 10, 15, 19, 21-25, 27, 31, 33, 37
government employees, 11, 25, 30
government functions, 9, 12, 15, 16
Government National Mortgage Association, 23
government operations, 1, 3

Government Performance and Results Act, 7, 13, 43
Government Printing Office, 16, 45
Government Reform and Savings Act, 5
government reform, viii, 3, 13, 16, 17, 19, 25, 45
government reinvention, viii, 21
government services, 4, 31
government work, 4, 13, 23, 30
governmental functions, 26, 28
Grace Commission, ix, x, 3
greater autonomy, 20, 31

H

helium reserves, 16
Heritage Foundation, 20
Higher Education Amendments of 1998, 27
high-risk federal functions, 43
House Government Reform and Oversight Committee, 14

I

implementation authority, 22
incentives, 12, 22, 36, 38
information technology, 1, 2, 12, 24, 44
initiative, 1, 28
innovation, 4, 10, 11, 36, 40, 42
Internal Revenue Service (IRS), viii, 5, 25, 26
investment, 5, 40, 41
Kettl, Donald, 12, 30, 35

L

leadership, 9, 24, 34, 37, 39
Line Item Veto Act, 13
localities, 15, 20

M

management practices, 12, 20
market terms, 22
means of implementation, 35
Merit Systems Protection Board, 39
modern human capital practices, 43

N

National Commission on Restructuring, 25
National Performance Review (NPR), v, vii, viii, 1, 4, 10, 11, 13-16, 18, 23, 34, 40, 41
National Technical Information Service, 23, 28
NPR recommendations, 3, 5, 6, 11, 12, 18, 20, 29, 34, 35, 38

O

Office of Management and Budget (OMB), x, 1, 2, 4, 6, 12, 15, 17, 30, 45
Office of Personnel Management (OPM), 2, 4, 23
Office of Student Financial Assistance (OSFA), 27
organizational culture, 11
organizational issues, 41
organizational performance, 27
organizational structures, 2, 18

P

Patent and Trademark Office (PTO), 23, 26- 28
Pentagon, 35, 39
performance-based organization(s) (PBO(s)), 20, 22, 23, 26-29, 31
personnel management, 2
personnel policy reforms, 20
personnel reductions, 20

petroleum reserves, 16
Postal Service, 5
power marketing administrations (PMAs), 16
President's Management Council (PMC), 4, 11
presidential memorandum, 4, 6
presidential orders, 38
private and public investment, 40, 41
private sector, 1, 3, 4, 14-16, 23, 41
privatization, 4, 15, 16, 43
procurement reform, 11, 20, 30, 38
productivity, 39, 40, 42
promote efficiency, 3, 4
proposed savings, 10
public administration, 3, 13, 40
public confidence problem, 39
public debt, 14
public management, 4, 42, 43
public sector enterprises, 3

R

Reagan, President Ronald, ix, 3, 37
redesign teams, 2
reduce costs, 4, 27
reducing government waste, 5
regulatory reform, 17
reinventing government, 5, 19, 22, 24, 39, 43
Reinventing Government, viii, 2, 11, 19-21, 23, 29, 30, 33, 35, 36, 38, 41
reinvention, viii, 2, 10, 19-21, 23, 24, 29-31, 35-39, 41
reorganization, vii, ix, 3, 5, 15, 17, 18, 33
Republican Congress, v, 13, 31, 35
Republican congressional leaders, vii, viii, 15, 16, 19
Republican majority(ies), 9, 13, 18
rural development, 5

S

Saint Lawrence Seaway Development Corporation, 23, 27
saving money, 9
savings, vii, x, 3, 10, 15, 16, 20, 30, 36, 40, 41
Seafood Inspection Program of the Department of Commerce, 23
Seafood Inspection Service, 28
Secretary of Education, 27
Social Security disability programs, 14
state and local government(s), 2, 10, 11, 14, 23, 29
streamlining initiatives, 10
systematic agenda, 41, 42

T

task force, vii, 1, 17, 45
tax policy, 25
taxpayer rights, 25
taxpayers, 25, 26
these broader political goals, 24

U

U.S. Army Corps of Engineers, 5
U.S. Customs Service, 5
U.S. Mint, 23, 28
unfounded mandates, 14
Unfunded Mandate Reform Act, 35

V

Vice President's Hammer Award, 36

W

Web site, 45
workforce, federal, 11, 35, 44